Garfield School Library   798
                                 Ra
Radlauer

Horsing around

DATE DUE

NO 26 '74			
DE 19 74			
JA 15 75			
MR 25 75			
AP 22 75			
MY 15 75			
SE 19 75			
NO 6 75			

horsing around

horsing around

by E. and R.S. Radlauer

illustrated with photographs by the authors

Franklin Watts, Inc., 845 Third Avenue, New York, N.Y. 10022
SBN 531-02034-7. Copyright © 1972 by E. and R. S. Radlauer
Library of Congress Catalog Card Number: 77-180241. Printed in the United States of America
2   3   4   5

Here's looking at you. Who's looking at you? Whoever it is, she's only using one eye. Well, you'll want more than one eye to see what we're going to see. It's called Horsing Around. There's no telling who thought up the name Horsing Around. But it's a good name because it tells how horses get around to doing some strange things.

Some people might go for dogs or cats. Dogs and cats are fine, but — you'd have a hard time Horsing Around on a dog or a cat. If you wanted to chase a bird or something, a dog or cat would be all right. In Horsing Around you have to use a horse or a **pony.** If you don't use a horse or a pony, you're just not horsing around.

4

Watch out! It's time to horse around. Keep your eyes open.

We wouldn't want you to get the idea that horsing around is just standing around looking at people with one eye or even two eyes. In some kinds of horsing around, we move around — like around the poles in a **pole bending** race. That's part of a big event called a **Gymkhana.** Just saying "Gymkhana" is an event in itself. In Gymkhana pole bending we travel around two poles spaced about 100 feet apart. The horse and rider travel around those poles at high speed. The rider who makes the trip in the shortest time wins. If the horse or rider touches or knocks over a pole, the **judge** adds two seconds to the rider's time.

Some riders can make a very fast pole bending trip. They stay close to the poles and still don't touch or knock any over. Then we have others who change the pole bending event into a horse bending game. Ouch! It just goes to show you that if a rider makes a turn around the pole too fast, she gets a chance to check up on the laws of **gravity.** The horse goes one way and the rider goes her own way — down — like parting company, you might say.

How many seconds does the judge add to your time when you stop to check the laws of gravity? That depends on how long you sit on the ground wondering what happened.

In a pole bending race the idea is *not* to bend a pole — or even touch it.

Pole bending is great — but horse bending — ?

Let's move along to the **barrel races.** Move along is right. We move fast and we're timed, the same as in the pole bending event. But in the barrel race we have to travel around all the barrels and make a tight circle around each barrel. It's in those tight circles that we have a little trouble. The really great riders don't slow down much going around the barrel. They just leave a circle of dust to show where they've been. It's all right for dust to touch the barrel. But if a horse or rider touches a barrel, the judge adds to the rider's timed run.

Is barrel racing a barrel of fun? Well, yes, until you touch or knock over a barrel.

Let's leave the Gymkhana pole bending and barrel racing circles and try a race with another kind of circle, a doughnut. Here we see fast galloping and fast doughnut gulping. We **gallop** from a **starting point** to a place we might call a doughnut point. At the doughnut point the rider gets off his horse and eats a doughnut that his friend is holding on a string.

After gulping the doughnut, the rider whistles, gets on his horse and gallops back to the starting point. The whistle shows the judge that the rider has swallowed all the doughnut. The fastest doughnut gulper-whistler-galloper wins the doughnut race. What does the galloping gulper win? How about another doughnut or maybe a stomachache?

The action in the egg-in-spoon race isn't to see how fast people can eat an egg. The eggs aren't even cooked and the race isn't a race. But we call it a race, anyway. It's a race where we try to keep our eggs from getting scrambled on the ground. While we hold an egg on a small spoon, the judge tells us to **walk, jog, lope,** or gallop. When we jog, lope, or gallop, we bounce. That makes the egg bounce.

The trick is to keep the egg in the spoon. The last one left in the race with an egg that isn't scrambled is the winner. What does the winner get? How about a dozen eggs? Or maybe a chicken?

The rules say the rider must eat all the doughnut.
Doesn't the horse get any?

There must be an easier way than this to carry
an egg.

A pajama race belongs in the horsing around action. But if you're in the race, you only get to wear pajamas for part of the time. It's a little bit like the doughnut race. We gallop from a starting point to a pajama point. As soon as you're at the pajama point, someone hands you a pair of pajamas. You put on the pajamas as fast as you can, get back on your horse, and gallop back to the starting point.

Sometimes it's hard to get pajamas on over the **riding clothes.** And sometimes, just for fun, someone will tie the pajama legs into knots. If you're in a hurry, the knots can slow you down by making you get caught half in and half out of the pajamas.

The fastest run in the pajama race wins. There are other things besides knots in the pajamas that can slow down a run. For one thing, there are some horses who don't like to be ridden by someone wearing pajamas. Even when a horse and rider are the best of friends, the sight of someone wearing pink pajamas will scare or **spook** a horse. So the horse has to do just what any spooked horse would do — try to run away. When a horse does that, maybe he's thinking about that story of long ago, the one about the headless horseman who rode at night to scare people.

If you're wearing pajamas, maybe you should be riding a nightmare.

Pajamas or not, you'd better not sleep while you're riding this horse.

When it comes to horsing around, the story of the headless horseman has to be one of the best. The story says that on Halloween night a rider came out carrying his head in his arms. That's some story, all right. We expect to see some strange things on Halloween night.

Then the story goes on to tell about how the headless horseman chased another rider. When he got near the rider he was chasing, he threw his head at him. That kind of horsing might be hard to believe.

Boy, that's using your head! But a guy could lose his head that way. Could that spook a horse?

Another horsing around story is about a rider named **Don Quixote.** He tried to be a knight. Only he wasn't quite a real knight. Real knights rode beautiful horses, went out to fight in wars, and saved ladies from great dangers.

Don Quixote was mostly a great danger to himself. To begin with he rode a **mule,** and instead of going into a war, he did his fighting with a windmill.

None of us think that fighting with a windmill should really be part of horsing around. But it doesn't hurt to dress up and ride like old Don Quixote, even if he was a little **squirrely** in the head.

14

Next time you have a headache, try this! It's a sure cure.

Here's Don Quixote getting ready to fight with a windmill — if he can find one.

When it comes to jumping, let's not get squirrely. You might say that there's nothing to jumping. All you have to do is get up and over the **crossbar** of the jump. Let's not forget that the horse and rider are supposed to finish the jump together. Even if the horse and rider finish the jump together, the crossbar is supposed to stay in place.

And we're all going to follow the jumping rule that says front legs over first and the rear legs will follow.

Here we are again, working on that law of gravity. Looks easy, doesn't it? Let's hold it while we check the **style.** Great, huh?

16

If the front legs go over, are the rear legs sure to follow?

Now, once you start a jump, you have to finish it. There's only one way to finish a jump — come down. Almost every jump looks great on the way up. There's all that sky ahead, the crossbar under the front legs, the rider up there, sitting pretty.

Jumps are like flying an airplane. Taking off is great. But landing is another problem. A jumping horse has landing problems, too. We have to bring all the weight back to the ground and at a pretty good speed, too. Ouch! Think of about 1,000 pounds of weight landing on two front legs. Ouch, again. Let's leave the jumping class to go to something slow, quiet, and easy.

Now, if we can get those rear legs back on the ground, the jump will be over.

Finding a place to horse around may be slow and quiet, but it isn't always easy. We can't horse around in the middle of a busy street or parking lot. That's why we all get together sometimes to try to save the places where we can horse around.

Some people don't understand how important it is to have some open spaces where we can do our racing, jumping, and doughnut eating. By getting together every once in a while we can show the people that houses, streets, stores, and roads are important. But we can show them that open spaces are important, too. After all, some people want a big open grassy place where they chase a little white ball into a hole in the ground. We all like a big open place where we can chase each other around, right?

Without a place to horse around, there wouldn't be any horsing around.

Merry-go-round horses have been chasing each other in circles for about two hundred years. Some people might say that a merry-go-round horse doesn't go anywhere but in a circle. But that's not true. The merry-go-round has gone all over the world.

Doesn't everyone want to ride a horse? Well, almost everyone. But not everyone can get to ride a real horse. So, there's the merry-go-round. Pick out the kind of horse you like, the color you like, and if you want it to go up and down or not.

Riding on the merry-go-round even has some of the same rules as riding a real horse. Watch where you're going, hold on, and sit up straight. Oh, yes, don't forget two more rules. Stay on until the horse stops and be careful when getting on or off a horse.

Merry-go-round horses horse around and around and around —

When it comes to getting off a horse, a **rodeo** has rules, too. In rodeo **bronco** riding, the rules say that a rider is supposed to stay on his horse. He's supposed to stay on for about seven seconds. Sometimes horses don't think this is such a good rule. After a two-second ride a horse might think it's time for the rider to get off. The rider wants to stay because the longer he stays on, the more **points** he gets.

So now we see how the rodeo bronco riding game works. The rider wants to stay on long enough to get points. The horse wants the rider off so he can be finished playing the bronco game. After finding out how bronco riding works, most people think they'd rather try their luck on a merry-go-round horse.

Here's another rule about horse riding. Well, it isn't exactly about riding, it's about how to get on and off a horse. A rider is supposed to get on and off a horse on the left side. You might think that people in a rodeo would forget this rule. Well, here's a bronco rider who remembered it, but he forgot the rule about waiting for the horse to stop.

Rules don't count when a horse and rider each start to go different ways. There's no telling which different way a bronco will go. But the rider, poor guy, there's only one way he can go — down. He hopes the horse will go away and not make **hoofprints** on his boots.

Don't tell anybody, but it could be get-off-your-horse time pretty soon.

You're right. It is getting-off time. Hey, horse, don't put any hoofprints on my boots.

ADRIAN PUBLIC SCHOOLS
Adrian, Michigan

Ever since anyone can remember, horses have been racing. And ever since anyone can remember, people have been **bet**ting on which horse will win a race. We all know that no one knows for sure which horse will win a race. But some people feel so sure that they will bet some money, or as we say, put money on the horse's nose, hoping that horse will be the first to put his nose across the **finish line.** If the horse wins, a person wins more money than he put on the horse's nose. If the horse doesn't win, then, you're right, the horse loses and so does the person who did the betting.

It's up to the **jockey** to make a horse want to win. A jockey who wins a lot gets to put on his **silks** and ride a lot. If a jockey loses all the time, no one bets on the horse he rides. He might even turn in his silks and go ride a merry-go-round horse.

Before each race, the horses parade around a place called a **paddock.** Then the jockeys **mount up** or get on their horses. The paddock parade gives the people a chance to look at the horses and jockeys. Some people think that looking at the horses and jockeys helps pick a winner. That might be true. Or it might be true that some people like green, so they bet on a horse with a jockey dressed in green silks. Other people will look right into a horse's eye. They think they can see the finish line in the horse's brain!

A lot of people don't bother to go to the paddock and look. They use their own brains to pick a lucky number. Some people say they would rather not bet on horses, just yet. They're waiting for the day when horses bet on people.

Look, it's the start of a race. Do you have any money on the winner's nose?

If you go to the paddock and a horse tells you he's going to win, you'd better believe it.

You don't bet on a tire race. You don't even go in a tire race unless the horse has been trained for it. In a tire race a horse and rider team tows a friend around the **course.** The friend rides on a tire. The course is marked by three poles. The team that covers the course in the shortest time is the winner.

This race doesn't have many rules. But one rule says that the horse and rider and the person on the tire must finish the race together. That shouldn't be too hard, or at least it shouldn't be too hard if the rider remembers to take the turns slowly. Going around a pole too fast could mean trouble.

Don't try this race unless the horse has been trained to pull a tire.

Here we have a person making a very close study of the ground. He didn't mean to make that close a study, but the horse and rider team got in too much of a hurry. They dumped him, so the team is out of the race.

Now we can see why the tire race has a rule about wearing a helmet. It's just the thing to wear for ground study. It keeps the rocks away. A helmet is also handy if the horse slows down and the rider on the tire keeps going. Coming up close enough to make a study of a galloping horse's hoofs could mean trouble. Maybe more trouble than going around a pole too fast.

What do the rules say about finishing the tire race with the tire rider sliding on his elbows? The rules don't say anything. If a rider wants to finish a race on his elbows, then good luck. Just bring on the stuff to patch up the elbows.

We don't think the team wanted to finish the race using the tire rider's elbows for skis. But if that's what they do, it's all right. The rules say the horse-rider-tire-rider must finish together. The rules don't say much about using elbows for skis.

This guy says it's fun. What do you think?

This may not be the best way to study rocks, but it will give you a close look.

Using elbows for skis isn't the best way to finish the tire race.

If you think horsing around looks like fun, you're right, most of the time. But a long time ago horsing around was more like work. Horses had to pull almost everything. One of the faster things horses used to pull was a **stagecoach.** The people on the stagecoach were just like people are now, always in a hurry. So the horses had to be big, strong, and fast.

Sometimes they had to be extra fast. That was when the coach was being chased by outlaws who wanted to rob the people in the coach. Outlaws knew that to catch a coach and rob it, they would have to ride faster horses than the ones pulling the coach.

The stagecoaches are gone from the roads, now. Where are the outlaws? Are they all on television? Some people say they're still around, only they don't ride horses anymore.

Outlaws get ready! Here comes the stagecoach.

Hey, wait! Maybe all the outlaws aren't gone from the roads. There are still some around — real bad 'uns, too. But what kind of outlaws stop on the road and leave clues for the **posse?** Well, that's part of the horsing around game called **Posse Pursuit.**

The outlaws, the bad 'uns, get a head start. Then after thirty minutes, the posse starts out to look for the outlaws. In this posse pursuit, the outlaws are on foot. If they can stay ahead of the posse for three hours and not get caught, then they go free. But they have to leave clues, like arrows, bits of cloth, or marks on the ground, for the riders in the posse to follow. Hey, posse! They went thataway! What way is thataway?

Now, to be in the posse pursuit, a horse and rider must be able to tell the bad guys from the good guys. Before starting the chase, it's a good idea to stop and look at the wanted posters. According to the posters we want Dirty Dan the Rat, Anna the Rotten Banana, Scribble the Kid, Robinette the Quick, and Nasty Nancina. And according to the posters they're wanted for such things as card cheating, train robbing, horse stealing. Well, card cheating is bad, train robbing is very bad, but horse stealing —! Any outlaw who does that must be caught.

Let's go. Everybody after Dirty Dan the Rat, Anna the Rotten Banana, Scribble the Kid, Robinette the Quick, and Nasty Nancina!

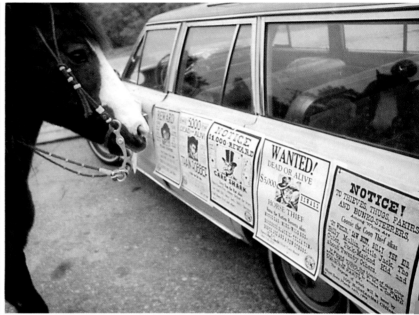

Hey, outlaws, you're supposed to run away with the money, not leave clues on the road.

If your picture shows up here, you're in trouble.

Ho! **Whoa!** Stop! Halt! Or whatever. Hey, everybody in the posse. Come here and look. It's a clue, an arrow, pointing down the road. Does that mean they went down the road? Probably not. Knowing those outlaws, it probably means they went left, right, or back. After all, they didn't get names like Dirty Dan, Anna the Rotten Banana, Robinette the Quick, or Nasty Nancina for nothing. You have to earn those names. So, now we know the truth.

It's hard work being an outlaw. You have to make a clue pointing one way, then go another way and hope to throw the posse off. Well, let's go get 'em. We'll go one way or the other way or another way. Well, some way we'll get those outlaws, or else!

Or else what? Or else we'll all meet this afternoon at the ice-cream parlor and have some ice cream. And since the posse couldn't catch the outlaws in time, who pays the bill at the ice-cream parlor? That's right. This time the posse buys for the outlaws. But next time, you outlaws, the posse will be smarter. They'll catch you.

But for now, the outlaws get to order ice cream. One fast serving of ice cream for Robinette the Quick, a double dish for Dirty Dan, ice cream covered with nuts for Nasty Nancina, triple scoops for Scribble the Kid. What about Anna the Rotten Banana — a banana split? No ice cream, thank you. Just a glass of water. Anna doesn't like ice cream.

Oh, come on — outlaws, clues, a posse and now this? Bring the biggest banana split of all for Anna the Rotten Banana! Here's one outlaw who earned it.

After them, everybody! They went thataway, or thataway, or thataway.

Being outlaws isn't so bad, after all.

You won't see any real outlaws in a parade, but you'll see some cowboys. They're probably not real cowboys. A real cowboy wouldn't load himself down with a lot of fancy **trappings.** But in a parade people like to see a rider loaded down with lots of silver and other trappings.

You know, those trappings cost plenty, like as much as $25,000. And the horse knows those silver trappings weigh plenty, like as much as 500 pounds.

A real working cowboy, the kind that chases cows, wouldn't want all that weight to carry when he's on the job. Besides, no real working cowboy would have the money for all those silver trappings. Or would he? Next time you see a cowboy, ask him — or ask his horse.

Well, you can tell this rider isn't dressed for a pajama race, that's for sure.

Just like in a parade, everyone in a horse show wants to look good enough to win a **trophy.** Horse shows are the part of horsing around that takes lots of training and lots of work. The rider has to train the horse to do the right things.

The judge in the show looks at how a rider **handles** his horse and how well the horse is **groomed.** For grooming we must have a horse clean, brushed, and wearing clean **tack.** Tack is what we call all the stuff the horse wears.

Some girls curl their hair before a show. Horses don't wear curled hair, but sometimes you'll see a horse with a braided **mane.** That's right. To win in a horse show, we'll even try a braided mane. But really, it's good riding that wins points toward winning a trophy.

Oh, come on, now. We go to all that trouble to look good for a horse show and what happens? Does any horse want to be in a show with *that* animal, whatever it is? We're supposed to chase those, remember? Getting trained, groomed, cleaned, and then lining up in a show with a cow, and a baby one at that, is just too much. Can it be true? Could that thing enter a barrel race? A tire race? Pull a stagecoach? Chase an outlaw?

Things are pretty bad when a cow enters a horse show. But if that thing, that cow, wins a trophy, it could be the end of horsing around. Whoever heard of a story called *cowing* around. Is this the end?

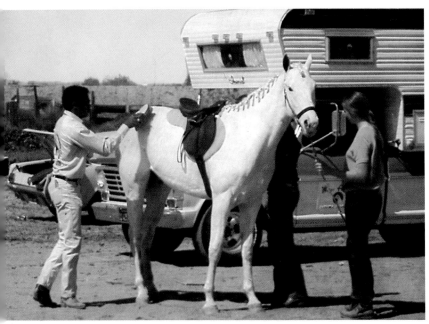

It takes an expert to get ready for a horse show.

Somehow there seems to be something wrong here, don't you think?

Well, yes, this is the end of the story about horsing around. But it's really more like the beginning, because it's where every story about horsing around starts. And there's a lot to learn.

Now, let's see, son. We'll start by learning about a doughnut race, then we'll talk about Don Quixote — Don, who?

Next we'll have to learn about jockeys and betting money. Also, son, you'll have to watch out for outlaws when you're on the Posse Pursuit. No, you don't need to be afraid of the outlaws. But the headless horseman! There's something to be spooked about. No, son, you'll never be on a merry-go-round. That's for another kind of horse. But if you are ever in a horse show with a cow, then that has to be the end.

42

Now, pay attention, son. There's a lot you have to learn about horsing around.

Glossary/Index

(Page number refers to the page
where the word first appears in the book)

45

46

Ruth and Ed Radlauer, authors of over fifty books for young people, are graduates of UCLA. They have worked as teachers, school administrators, reading specialists, and instructors in creative writing. Their books have been in the areas of science, language, social studies, and, more recently, high-interest reading materials. The books in the Sports Action series are *On the Drag Strip, Scramble Cycle, Horsing Around*, *Buggy-go-Round, On the Sand, Chopper Cycle, Salt Cycle, Motorcycle Mutt, Bonneville Cars, On the Water, Foolish Filly,* and *Racing on the Wind.*

Along with their three children, two horses, a dog, and an ancient cat, the Radlauers live in La Habra, California.